With love to Matilda

A TEMPLAR BOOK

First published in the UK in hardback in 2002 by Templar Publishing
This edition published in 2003 by Templar Publishing,
an imprint of The Templar Company plc,
Pippbrook Mill, London Road, Dorking, Surrey, RH4 1JE, UK
www.templarco.co.uk

Distributed in the UK by Ragged Bears Ltd.,
Ragged Appleshaw, Andover, Hampshire, SP11 9HX

First softback edition

ISBN 1-84011-535-1

Edited by Marcus Sedgwick
Designed by Mike Jolley

Printed in Belgium

THE COCKEREL and the FOX

Retold & illustrated by HELEN WARD

templar publishing

Over the rolling hills, beyond the wood, there was once a small farm. Ringed about by fields and gardens it stood quietly, one springtime morning. No-one was yet awake. The birds still slept in their nests, the farmer in his bed. But then...

A "Cock-a-Doodle-Doo!" rang out,
and then again, and again, rolling out loudly down the valley.
It was Chanticleer, the cockerel; herald of the morning,
pride of the farmyard, rustling his fine feathers
as he crowed in the day.

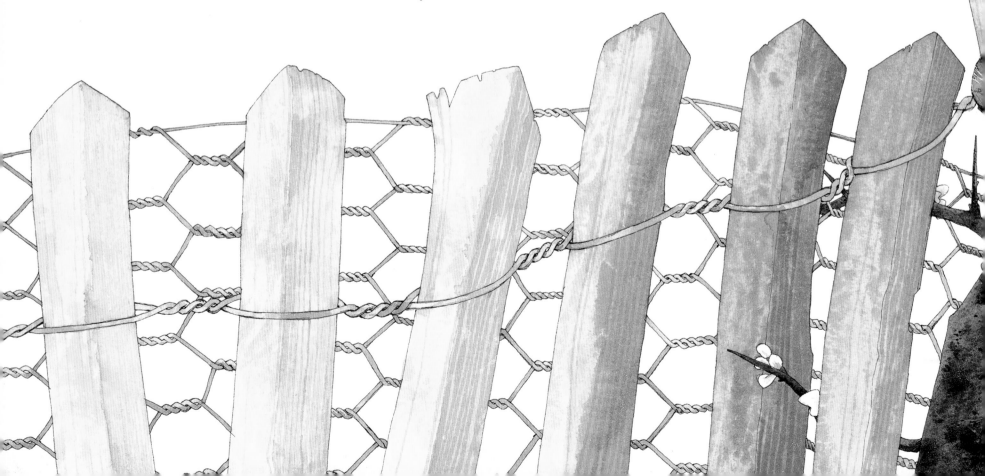

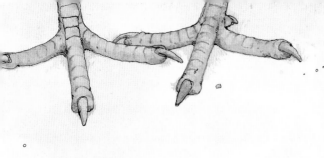

His mate, a pretty hen named Pertelote, looked on admiringly,

for Chanticleer was so handsome, so proud, so loved by all.

However, Chanticleer was vain too. He often thought

how fine he looked, how much he was admired,

but, as they say, pride comes before a fall...

One morning Chanticleer awoke, trembling with fear.

He had dreamed a terrible dream, of a reddish, doggish,

snarling beast, with ears and nose

and claws and teeth...

...all sharply pointed!

Was it a warning?

"No, no, my dear," soothed Pertelote,

"a nightmare.

It will soon be forgotten."

And so it was...

A month later at dawn,
something pushed through
the hedge…

and lurked among the cabbages till noon. It was Mr Fox — reddish, doggish and hungry for his supper.

Chanticleer, strutting on the fence, had never seen a fox before and nearly squawked when one slid up beside him. But Mr Fox was quick to put him at ease. "I apologise, Mr Cockerel Sir," said the fox, "I don't mean to be alarming, but I heard that voice of yours and it really is quite charming."

"Won't you stretch your neck up high
and crow **again for me?**"

Chanticleer was glad to oblige.

He threw back his head and shut his eyes,

determined to crow his loudest.

"Cock-a-Doodle-...

Squawk!" In a foxy flash Chanticleer found himself held by the throat.

"A fox! A fox!" screeched Pertelote. "A fox is stealing my love!"

Her cries rang round the farmyard.

"Foul murderer!" clucked the flustered hens...
and stirred the bumbling bees, and woke the dogs from
dreaming sleep. "Stop thief!" quacked the anxious ducks
and set the geese a-honking.

The noise summoned the pigs
and the piglets too,
the ewes and lambs,
but all too late -

for the fox and his prize

had slipped beneath the gate.

In the field the cows

and their calves took up the chase,

and soon it seemed the whole farmyard was on Mr Fox's tail.

"Stop the fox!" they cried,

as they neighed and brayed their way across the field.

"Save our Chanticleer!"

Then Mr Fox reached the edge of the murky wood.

What dangers lurked in the shadows? What waited beyond

the safety of the farmyard and fields? The animals stopped.

None dared go near. The chase was over.

But Chanticleer still had life and breath and,

better still, the chase had given him time to think...

"Mr Fox," he rasped. "I have to admit you **are** a clever fellow. Such bravery and wit! It's such a shame these lowly beasts do not realise. You should tell them what a fine trick you played on me! What a cunning plot you devised! After all, they think that I am the cleverest creature in all the kingdom..."

And Mr Fox, keen to make the matter clear, opened his stupid mouth to speak...

"Beware of false flattery,"
clucked the wiser Chanticleer,
safe in a high tree.
"Now there is a moral worth remembering!"

And with the briefest of nods the fox
turned and slunk away through the
murky wood, his stomach
rumbling all the way.

A FEW WORDS ABOUT
THE STORY

This story is best known from its appearance in *The Nun's Priest's Tale* in Geoffrey Chaucer's *Canterbury Tales*, but tales about foxes and cockerels have a long pedigree. *The Cockerel and the Fox* appears in La Fontaine's fables of the 17th century, but similar tales exist as far back as Aesop's fables of ancient Greece.

The cunning fox has been outwitting his neighbours and his enemies for thousands of years. In the 6th century BC Aesop told of the fox who tricks a crow into dropping the cheese held in his beak, by flattering him into singing. Closer to the present story, Aesop also tells of *The Dog, the Cockerel and the Fox*, in which the Cockerel outwits the Fox, with the aid of his friend, the Dog.

Many of Aesop's fables seem to have originated in Africa and were told in ancient Greece before being lengthened and retold by travelling storytellers and minstrels in Europe. The fox tales were gathered together in the medieval French epic, the *Roman de Reynart*, written in the late 12th century by Pierre de Saint Cloud. The stories, which later became known as *Reynard the Fox* in English, concern the clever tricks and mischievous adventures of the eponymous fox, and contain the adventure that Chaucer used for the tale told by the nun's priest in his *Canterbury Tales*.

Chaucer began to write *The Canterbury Tales* in 1387. The tales are presented as a series of stories told in a competition devised to help pass the time by a group of pilgrims making their way to Canterbury.

Chaucer had travelled widely in Europe as a diplomat and a soldier. He had met influential people and had access to some important libraries. The stories in his tales were collected from his experiences, and the story of Chanticleer, the proud but vain cockerel who is both outwitted by and ultimately outwits the treacherous fox, is one of these.

The fox as a character has lasted because he is a most beguiling anti-hero. He is cunning, charming and adaptable, and able to talk himself out of (and sometimes into) trouble. He has far too many vices, few virtues and in his history has outwitted the king of the beasts and peasant alike.

Chanticleer is the epitome of nobility and duty (if a little stupid). He cares for and protects his wives and children. In a community without clocks his crowing starts and regulates the day. Chaucer's Chanticleer has such a grasp of the sun's movement throughout the sky that he crows accurately upon the hour. And though initially fooled by the fox's trickery, he finally beats the fox at his own game.

These ancient animal stories are always open to re-interpretation. This, and the fact that the fundamental moral lessons they contain have not changed, has helped to ensure their survival over hundreds, if not thousands of years.

So remember: beware of flattery, keep your eyes open and do not speak without thinking first!

THE RARE BREEDS

His mate, a pretty hen named Pertelote...

All domestic poultry are descended from the Asian Red Jungle Fowl. Over many years they were selectively bred to become hundreds of varieties of birds. Modern farming methods, concentrating on a few intensively reared strains, have led to the rapid disappearance of the barnyard breeds.

1. Welsumer – derives its name from the Dutch village of Welsum from where it was exported in the early part of the 20th century. Famous for its dark brown eggs.
2. Dorking – a very ancient breed, described by the Romans as long ago as AD 47. Peculiar for the fact they have five toes – most chickens having only four.
3. Ancona
4. Leghorn
5. Frizzel

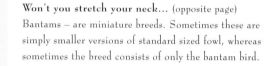

Won't you stretch your neck... (opposite page)

Bantams – are miniature breeds. Sometimes these are simply smaller versions of standard sized fowl, whereas sometimes the breed consists of only the bantam bird.

This illustration features many bantam varieties:
1. Silver Quail Barbu D'Anvers (Belgian), bantam
2. Blue (laced) Orpington, bantam
3. Silver Spangled Hamburgh, bantam
4. Salmon Faverolles, bantam
5. Double-laced Barnvelder, bantam
6. Buff Sussex, bantam
7. Wheaten Old English Game, bantam
8. Speckled Sussex, bantam
9. Black Scots Dumpy, bantam
10. Jubilee Indian Game, bantam
11. Gold Sebright, bantam
12. Black Wyandotte, bantam
13. Barred Wyandotte, bantam
14. Gold Partridge Dutch, bantam

The illustration also depicts three standard sized fowl:
15. Appenzeller Spitzhaubens
16. Brahma, light
17. Cochin, buff

Others

18. Guinea fowl – originated on the Guinea Coast of Africa, hence their name. They were frequently imported into Britain via Turkey and thus became known as "Turkeys." Confusingly however, this is not the bird we know today as the turkey!

8. Silky – thought to have originated in Asia, they are well-known for their excellence at sitting, and will hatch ducklings or geese as happily as their own eggs!

Geese – It is believed that almost all domestic geese are descended from the wild Greylag Goose.

9. Chinese

10. Brecon Buff – the first buff-coloured breed, created in Wales in 1934 from the geese on the local Breconshire farms.

Ducks

11. Crested – have always been a rare breed. They come in almost any colour and are renowned for the crest of feathers on the top of their heads.

12. Trout Indian Runner – exported from Malaya in the 1870s, the Indian Runner is an elegant bird well-known as an excellent layer of large eggs. They come in many colours; as well as the Trout, here are the Chocolate (13) and Fawn and White (14).

15. Silver Appleyard, drake – named after their creator, Reginald Appleyard, who created this breed in Suffolk, UK in the 1930s, the bird is a good layer of eggs, and very friendly.

16. Guinea fowl

19. Turkey – when the Pilgrim Fathers first landed in America, they named the large birds they found there Turkey, after the "Turkey" Guinea Fowl which they resembled, and this is the breed with which we are now familiar.

20. Pigeons

Goats

21. Golden Guernsey Goat– one of three 'Golden Breeds' of Guernsey. The Cow, famous for its creamy milk, is known throughout the world, but there was also a Golden Guernsey Donkey, now extinct. The Goat is a very rare breed, and nearly became extinct during the Second World War when the Channel Islands were occupied by German forces.

"A fox, a fox!" (right)

1. Brown-breasted Oxford Old English Game – of ancient English origin. The word 'Game' in their name hints at the fact that they were bred originally to fight – cock fighting was a popular sport for hundreds of years, and was only made illegal in Britain in 1849, more as a result of the anarchy that accompanied a fight than for any great concern for the bird's welfare.

2. Fayoumi

3. White-crested Black Poland – these birds have spectacular crests, in a variety of colours, and were common across Europe, 'Poland' being a misnomer.

4. Dorking

5. Welsumer

6. Buff Orpington

7. Gold Brahma

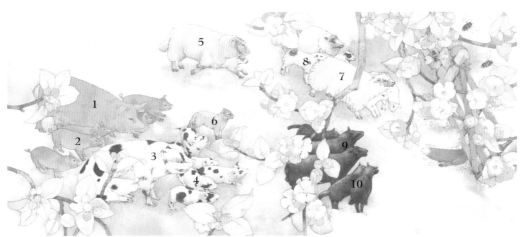

The noise summoned the pigs... (above)

Domestic swine of prehistoric times roamed through the forest and would have frequently mated with wild boar. More recently, efforts were made to improve them by interbreeding with breeds from the Far East.

1. Tamworth and piglets (2) – one of the breeds least influenced by the Far Eastern imports, the Tamworth as a result produces relatively small litters of 7 or 8 piglets. The breed has done well in Australia, however, due to its resistance to sunburn.

3. Gloucestershire Old Spot and piglets (4) – thrive outside, and produce large litters, but do not do well indoors, becoming too fat. As a result, they are now a very rare breed.

Sheep

5. Portland and lambs (6) – according to some, the ancestors of the breed swum ashore from a Spanish ship, sunk during the Armada. Although it is true that the Portland does contain Spanish blood, this is most probably due to trade, rather than strong-swimming, Spanish ship-wreck-surviving sheep!

7. Wensleydale and lambs (8) – famous for their rich wool that grows in long ringlets, their milk was once used to make Wensleydale cheese.

9. Black Welsh Mountain and lambs (10) – one of the varieties of the Welsh Mountain – the others being the fantastically named Badger-faced Torddu, the Torwen and the Balwen.

In the field the cows and their calves... (below)

Cattle – all breeds of cattle are descended from the prehistoric wild Aurochs, long since passed into extinction.

1. Belted Galloway – originally from the south-west of Scotland, in winter the breed has a long coat suitable for such a challenging environment. Their name derives from the large belt of white around their bellies.

2. Gloucester and calf (3)

4. Highland and calves (5) – with a thick woolly undercoat this is another breed which is well adapted to survive in the cold and wet winters of the Scottish Highlands.

6. British White

7. British Longhorn – the breed bears a remarkable similarity to the type of cattle depicted on the walls of stone age caves. They were once widely kept for their versatility, being as useful pulling a wagon as they were providing plentiful milk.

Sheep

8. Cotswold – this breed once inhabited the Cotswold hills in their thousands, although it was the sheep that gave its name to the hills, not the other way round. 'Cots' were the sheep pens that were dotted along the 'Wolds' – the bare hills of this part of southern Britain.

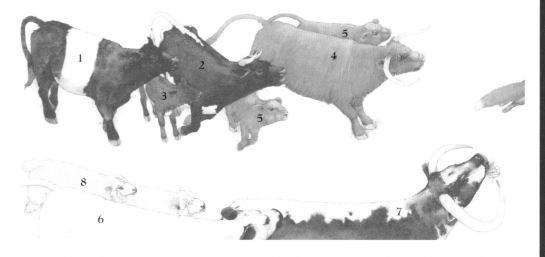

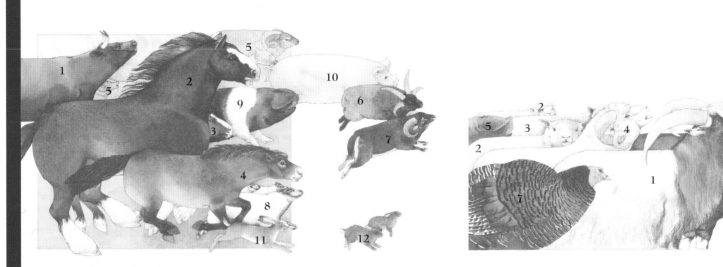

"Stop the fox!" (above)

Cattle

1. Kerry cow

Horses

2. Shire and foal (3)

4. Exmoor pony

Sheep

5. Castlemilk Moorit, ram

6. Four-horned Hebridean – the Hebridean can grow two, four, or even six horns! It is believed that the breed originated with the Vikings, who introduced the animal to places as far apart as Iceland and North Africa.

7. Soay – the ancestors of all modern sheep, they have changed little since the Stone Age, living on the remote islands of Soay and Hirta off the west coast of Scotland.

8. Badger-faced Torddu Welsh Mountain

Pigs

9. Wessex Saddleback – despite a reputation as a good all round breed, producing large litters, plentiful milk and being good mothers, this pig is now very rare.

10. Middle White – bred originally as a pork-producing animal, the Middle White has a short snub nose as a result of crosses with Chinese stock in the 18th century.

Others

11. Hare

12. Rabbits

Then Mr Fox reached the edge... (below)

Cattle

1. Highland

2. White Park, bull – now an 'ornamental' breed, once used by Druids and Romans for religious ceremonies.

Pigs

3. Large Black

Horses

4. Suffolk Punch

Sheep

5. Herdwick

"Mr Fox," he rasped. (above)

Goats are well-known for their capacity to eat almost anything, being able to digest many plants that other animals cannot.

1. Bagot – the ancestors of the breed were exported from the Holy Land after Richard the Lion Heart's crusades in the 12th century.

Sheep

2. Ryeland

3. Down – reared as the meat breeds of the farming industry, their wool is crimped in appearance.

4. Merino

Pigs

5. Large Black

6. Berkshire

Poultry

7. Turkey

8. Welsumer